Touch

George Bowering

Touch

selected poems 1960-1970

McClelland and Stewart Limited
Toronto/Montreal

Publication of this book was assisted
by a grant from the Canada Council

0-7710-1596-8

The Canadian Publishers
McClelland and Stewart Limited
25 Hollinger Road, Toronto 374

for CO, RD, & RC

*the flowers
from the shore,*

*awakened
the sea*

Acknowledgements

Most of these poems are from some of my earlier books: *Sticks & Stones* (Tishbooks), *Points on the Grid* (Contact Press), *The Man in Yellow Boots* (Ediciones el Corno), *The Silver Wire* (Quarry Press), *Baseball* (Coach House Press), *Rocky Mountain Foot* (McClelland & Stewart), *The Gangs of Kosmos* (House of Anansi), & *Sitting in Mexico* (Imago).

"The Owl's Eye," was a broadsheet, *The Orange Bear Reader* 7. The first section of "Poem Written for George (2)" was a poster from Quarry Press.

"Round Head," & "Play Among the Stars" were publisht in the anthology, *Inside Outer Space*, edited by Robert Vas Dias, Doubleday, 1970.

The rest of the poems were publisht in the following magazines: *Ahora*, *The Ant's Forefoot* (ed. by David Rosenberg), *Black Moss*, *Imago*, *Is* (ed. by Victor Coleman), *Noose*, *The Open Letter* (ed. by Frank Davey), & *0 to 9*.

In True Diction

A few years ago, when Jack McClelland suggested doing a Selected Poems I said naw I'm too young. So later it was suggested that instead of a Selected Poems I could do a selected poems & I agreed, the purpose being to get back into print some of the older pieces that were publisht by the gracious little presses I have been happy to work with. What you hold here is not a representative collection–my poems for the past decade have grown longer & longer, until now nearly all I work on are books themselves. I didnt think it right to take any bites out of any of these latter, *George*, *Vancouver*, or *Genève*, or my *Autobiology*, for instances. Bad enough to slice segments from the suites called *Rocky Mountain Foot* & *Sitting in Mexico*. I have reprinted a short book, *Baseball*, & decided to leave out another, *Two Police Poems*. What you hold is a selection of some poems, short & middle-distance, that I publisht in my first decade.

The question rose: how do I pick out a minority of my verses? You can choose the best or you can choose the ones you like best or you can choose the ones that best exhibit what you believe about poetry. But what is the first, how can you do the second, & why should the third not be everything. I abandoned the plan of any set guideline & fell to typing out my strophes & let's see, what will happen on the way to a book full. It happened that most of the poems are from the early sixties because it takes time for poems to get publisht. Okay. It also happened that quite a few are anthology pieces–I can be influenced by critics & editors. & it happened that more than half of my list of titles could be found in the list of titles Angela made up. Good.

So the poems you have. I would like you to read them aloud, hearing that punctuation, including the line-ending, is part of the composition. A woman in Barrie told me that she didnt like my poetry before she came to my reading & then she liked it–that was because she hadnt really read it, not all of what she had. If you read aloud you can hear the rime, & rime well used is punctuation too. Please use it well & we will work to gather, & we will play together.

Montreal,
GB, Feb 71

As Introduction

I lie to you
as often as I lie to myself

& to all of them
I speak to as you.

As your-self
comes to me, finally

only as I will permit,
with truth I'll permit.

Who said I have to tell
truth, making songs?

Well, I did,
but–

Any music will touch us
as its power is allowed.

Is allowable.
Listen here not for truth

but the shapeliness
of the lies.

Let our world
lie in this relaxation.

Locus Solus

Attaching toes to Vancouver downtown sidewalks over-
sluiced with rain water
                    under billowed concave black
umbrella dripping around me
                        eye down on neon reflections
wiggled in the gutter
                    cursing & moving alone
next to shoulders of down looking strangers
soggy in the rain

I remember dried out lips & tongue
                        long trip without water-
bottle down the side of old Blue Mountain

It was a hundred & twenty
                       in the shade
                       but there was no shade
& coming down was harder than going up
down in the empty water-
drainage slashes
                       in dust now
                       & over boulder slides
Finally down
to lichen green rocks
                       & face first into the stream muddied
                       by the dog a few yards up
head pusht into the water
teeth aching & belly pulled tight by the cold sucking down the throat
& the final walking home
                       respecting the sun & taking it easy
                       planting feet in long easy strides

Walking Poem

One step two steps
                    from the avenue
where I live—

trees lining me
walking within
the margins of the mind

three steps then
                    a
cross the street
dodging hard driven cars

            Thinking what?
            happens in the
            swing from one
            step to touch
            of the next–

dogged steps then
thinking
            what?
happens to be the way I walk
on the avenue where I live

Family

Was there power where I sprang from?
I wonder
             over the pondering of my past,
it must have begun with
                         hairpants prowlers of an earlier
Angle Land.   Picts, Jutes, Scots, carrying my seeds over a foggy
Island.   Families of Og, joining me to the Dukes of
Happy Land.

          Rich man
          poor man
          beggar man

          thief

In the descent & climbing, a tangled rime of time.

I know there was a singer of hymns in the centuries
& a peerage visited upon us.
                         & kings related & stories
told by idiots in stone houses.
                         Under thatcht roofs, others–
Sibilant growing of the Church & Nation
                              & the Clan.

To where we are, now.
                    No power but the delta of time.
No past unfogged on the Island.
                         No family but me.

Grandfather

Grandfather
          Jabez Harry Bowering
strode across the Canadian prairie
hacking down trees
                    & building churches
delivering personal baptist sermons in them
leading Holy holy holy lord god almighty songs in them
red haired man squared off in the pulpit
reading Saul on the road to Damascus at them

Left home
          big walled Bristol town
at age eight
               to make a living
buried his stubby fingers in root snarled earth
for a suit of clothes & seven hundred gruelly meals a year
taking an anabaptist cane across the back every day
for four years till he was whipt out of England

Twelve years old
                    & across the ocean alone
to apocalyptic Canada
                    Ontario of bone bending labor
six years on the road to Damascus till his eyes were blinded
with the blast of Christ & he wandered west
to Brandon among wheat kings & heathen Saturday nights
young red haired Bristol boy shoveling coal
in the basement of Brandon college five in the morning

Then built his first wooden church & married
a sick girl who bore two live children & died
leaving several pitiful letters & the Manitoba night

He moved west with another wife & built children & churches
Saskatchewan Alberta British Columbia Holy holy holy
lord god almighty
                    struck his labored bones with pain
& left him a postmaster prodding grandchildren with crutches
another dead wife & a glass bowl of photographs
& holy books unopened save the bible by the bed

Till he died the day before his eighty fifth birthday
in a Catholic hospital of sheets white as his hair

The Descent

When I think of him
it is me–

as old pictures
in boxes
–old books covered with
dust & cobwebs
old hockey sticks, baseball gloves
college annuals!

have been carried
from house to house
& I turn them over
many forgetful hours underground
his handwriting from
–how many?
thirty years ago?

the eyes in the pictures
straight without desire
–like mine

it is me in
outlandish clothes, long wool
bathing suit, plus-fours, white
shoes, holding tennis raquet

me staring fixedly at the invisible
rigid camera

beside a jazzy black car
with white canvas top
spoke wheels resting on dusty road

somewhere nineteen twenty-seven Okanagan
highway beside rocky blasted cliff
over dangerous drop into water below

In one family picture he is bald
having shaved his head

for fun & the summer
sunshine–my grandmother
         told me, tho she never

laught, she would have thought
         it funny if she wasnt
a Baptist–

             his brother's collie
dog sitting beside him, muzzle
         in his hand. Old collie
dead how many years, &

my grandmother, & who
         knows where the picture
is now? What happens to old

cars? I remember automobile
         graveyards beside the highway
all the way down the coast

one summer–But I wander–what
         about him? Where did he
drive to? I know he had to go

         out of the house to have a
cigarette. There were many verbs around
         that house, & the chief among

         them was Give Thanks. Well,
I hear he drove thru the snow
         forty miles for a cold

         basketball game, where you
could work it out in sharp turns
         leg-weary dashes up the floor

         while Llew, older, lay at home
on his broken back, painting
         in oils, pleasant scenes, giving

thanks. Or Gerry, behind the
shed, trying to roll cigarettes from
        apple leaves. Ella cheering without

    knowledge when he scored a
basket from far out. "A point for
        us!"–give thanks.

    An entirely masculine gesture, scoring
a basket. I remember where they
        lived you had to go out of

    the house to have a crap sometimes
in the frozen middle of winter
        exposed girls & boys alike.

Well, when I look at the pictures I
        see me looking back, giving thanks
to my twenty-first year, till I

    gave up praying. He was a young
man at college, he got up in the
        dawn light, walkt thru frozen

snow to light the coal furnaces, the
        funny feeling you get all alone
in the forbidden early part of the

    day. You hear animals grunting like
people against the warmth of walls,
        see birds balancing sleepy &

frouzzle-feathered on wires, making the
        first morning slant-light gray peeps
& chirrups, answers coming quietly

    from down the line. It was
like that the summer we watcht for
        fires together on top of a mountain

—he crackt ice for the morning coffee
    & the slippery porridge, & birds
made tentative forbidden sounds

    from another part of the forest.
& sometimes I'd find the pictures from
    that summer—me stirring the grouse

in the pot—or him bending over in
    undershirt straps, hands on knees
civilized man in whiskers, grimacing

    on top of a mountain, the dog
somewhere yapping at a chipmunk
    tail full of burrs, which we

would stop to pick out, quietly, while
    the sun got warmer on our backs,
the tent, getting near time for him to

    check the other mountains for smoke.
Both of us wandering the top of our
    mountain in underwear & pyjamas.

    With the pictures, old love letters,
magazines, college annuals, calendars with
    circled dates, & the hopeless worn out

pages of labor songs, that I never askt
    about, strange relics of the nineteen
twenties, him alive during Dempsey &

    Sacco Vanzetti times—so did he? walk
in crowds singing those things? detach
    himself in thoughtful rooms, reading them?

    Oh my darling Nelly Gray
    They have taken you away
    & I'll never see my
    Sweetheart any more—

is what I heard, mornings of slippers
& banging stove lids I'd awaken
        to see my giant icicle still outside

    the window, & him in the kitchen
crumpling newspapers & rattling the
        woodbox, rolling cigarette while the
flames caught, always the first time.

        To which I have always aspired.
Walking now to the kitchen mornings with
        the same gait of bony feet, slippers

making the same first scratching sounds of
        morning, woman in bed–depending
–I could run a mountain top alright.

        Reading as much as I can. His old
books–Huxley, Taine, Hardy, Wells, Dickens,
Crane–dusty volumes in dirty boxes all

signed how many?–thirty-five years
        ago? Thought Control, Speedwriting,
Mysteries of the Yoga, Scott to Antarctica, the

        Sun and its Neighbours, Food for Thought,
Western Grain Farmer, the Life Bounteous,
        Fertility Cults among the South Sea

Islanders. Pages spiderwebbed together. Book
        marks from Brandon Manitoba shops
where I passt thru once, looking for

        designs of age in the trees, imagining
freezing walks to the basement furnaces,
        long hours of warming air, waking birds.

        –the descent follows the ascent–to wisdom
        as to despair

                              —gave up praying
as his father before him? I dont know
        when, but in the pictures he is youth

leader bent on ethics & behavior thru the
        world, high scorer on basketball team,
top scholar, lost his forefinger in a buzz

        saw, left pictures, cars, church, behind
him, gave thanks, climbed the mountain
        of solitude, spoke sometimes in short

burst of poetry, trimming the muscles of his
        arm, building houses & filling them.
Leaving the rest in the basement, dusty &

        remembered, behind years of worn out shoes,
where I find it all now, it is me
        when I think of him, him—me—we—

        —the descent follows

live again but not as his mother told us,
        he descends, remembers, lives again, in
me, ascending from this basement, into

        a new life, reborn, from him, from time, out
into the air, shaking off the dust like a
        dust-rolling dog, free, to wisdom & despair—

For WCW

Language lifted
      out of the ordinary
           into the illumination
of poetry.
             Objects: sticks & stones
                  coming together
you place before
      our eyes
           exposed bare to the weather
rained on &
      crackt dry in the sun

A stick a stone
      a river cutting thru clay
a white barn in a field
      a cat coiled
          on a box

Words
      coming together
          moving at one another
traction for the tongue

      Look at that!   American
language shouting
      across the Potomac
          ring coins over the river
open out western states
      –anywhere a man can
          hear his voice

      In the machines of Paterson
rattling ten million words a day
      a voice moves
          physical–not understood
      as lit-er-ary, but moving

      as a machine, with traction
fitting itself against resistance

–Song understood by
            the banging ear

II

A sparrow
balances in the wind

voicing song
into the shifting air

It is a small thing
but big as all creation

to its mate beside it
on the wire, balancing

The wind blows
the wire snaps underfoot

the feet hold
the feathers have no time

to compose themselves

It is
as it should be or
as it is

III

I heard he askt the excavators
                    for a boulder
        dumpt in his
                front yard

They must have thought
                he was some old nut

I mean you dig a boulder
                  out of the ground you dont
            leave it in your front yard

I mean what good is a big rock?
            all you can do
                is look at it
            or lean on it

I mean if youve got a lawn
                  youve got to mow around
                    the damn thing
                  & clip the bloody grass

I mean I hear he used to be
                a doctor, what'd he do
        with the gallstones he cut out
                put them on the bloody mantel?

IV

The descent beckons
        as the ascent beckoned
                I understand that

till the point of
        What now?
                He is dead gone forever

& to where?
        Into that black which is
                blacker than the memory
of black?
        It is as it should be
                or as it is.

He is a part of the history
        he brought poems together
                clutcht out of chaos

he will be the reason
        behind a language where
                epics can be clutcht

he will be sticks & stones
        hewer of wood
                drawer of water

                William
                        Carlos
                                Williams

Steps of Love

Coming out of your clothes you were
girl in the night
                    naked in a strange house
                    receptive to a question
                    of what I would do

you were for the first time
uncovered to me
your two white shoulders thin in the air
huncht & shining there

& breast turning to me
cool skin of unimagined girl suspended in shadow
& hands now bashful
searching for a place to rest behind you

            You listened to my silence

            you gathered something in your mind

            & you danced on your bare feet

            with your long arms to meet me

Rime of Our Time

Here is Angela's
hair on the side of
my face; love as

clean & soft as
it is immediate
to me. Two heads

on a pillow faces to-
gether eyes closed or
open in the dark.

Time is on our side
now no trick to
scrutinize but behind

us days. Accumulating
sounds we make in
our sleep, our dreams

of one another seen.

For A

what joy
to teach you joy
of love

a little
at a time

what fun too
our one
little find
at a time

how dear
the simpleness
of it

how thank you
how thank me

for each
syllable
we say of it

Inside the Tulip

Inside the tulip
we make love
on closer look
seeing faint green lines, new

Let me share this flower
with you, kiss you
press my tongue on pollen
against the roof of my mouth

Look at me long enough
& I will be a flower
or wet blackberries dangling
from a dripping bush

Let me share you
with this flower, look
at anything long enough
& it is water

on a leaf, a petal
where we lie, bare legs together

The Snow

(for Robert Kelly)

1.

The snow now
low in the sky

the snow, spread out
is energy, winter light

sign of white
world bird, spread wings

The snow
does not clasp

it falls away
from foot steps

a light spray
of energy, soundless

as the crackling
of the sun

2.

The bird, wings spread
is winter

Earth is round
the bird, coming to earth

soundless, does not clasp
its wings rest

over the round earth
a winged caress

The sun now, low
too far away to be heard

The Grass

I must tell you
of the brown grass
that has twenty times
this year, appeared
from under the
melting snow, reared
its version of spring
like a sea lion coming
out of water, a-dazzle
in the sun, this
brave grass the sun
will only burn again
returning like a tiny
season.

Moon Shadow

Last night the rainbow
round the moon

climbed with how sad steps
as I walkt home

color surrounding me
cloud around my head.

> I am moon!
> Arrows fly at me!
>
> I slide cold & pale
> over cold earth
> of Alberta winter!
>
> I show one face
> to the world,
> immaculate still,
> inscrutable female
> male animal ball
> of rock
> shining with borrowed light
>
> rolling in that light
> the other side of
> forgetful space!

I am a shining tear
of the sun

full moon, silver,
who but myself knows
where the sun shall set?

I am able to instruct
the whole universe,

instruct the heart,
the weeping eye
of any single man.

Slide over the moon-
lit earth, a shadow
of a chariot.

       Walk homeward
forgetful where I have been

with how sad steps
my shadow before me

on the earth, moon shadow
rainbow round my heart,
wondering where in the universe I am.

Far from the Shore

Is he dead? Is my friend dead?
Crasht, face against painted steel,
splattered with blood & needles of glass,
broken head splotcht with oily blood,
crusht bug of pavement-grinding crash,
lost coat & necktie twisted in mud?

Where is he now? That I hear his voice
        in my ear, urging he is alive, gentle face
    needing shave somewhere on land, white teeth
smiling at a world of air. Those teeth
        broken into half-rotted jags, strewn
    by uncaring night time hand, somewhere.

In a sky-blue casket, cast into the ground–
someone saw it, saw them do it, told me:
        I cant deny that, I cant deny last summer
    when I bought him a bottle of whiskey,
waved him away in Vancouver night,
the last time I saw him, away in a car,
        later off, to Ontario, what bleary clime.

& one month ago, filtered word, unwilling
    news, he is killed in auto wreck on far
        foreign highway–what sudden loom
    in front of night, blazing lights in eyes,
desperate jag of heavy car, then, now,
        horrid air-filling explosion, shrieking steel,
            awkward shrapnel gouging into ground, a
twirling upside down rubber wheel, sirens.

All in the silence of my night here
    two thousand highway miles West, he was
often drunk, lay on floor at parties, eyes glazed
in utter joy & defiant empty bottle a scepter
    in his drunken white kingly hand, amused
        to the edge of his mouth, teeth in a second
    a light on his unshaven face, my friend,
        now mouldering–agh!–in the ground–

Handled by family & deacon, churchmen,
   professionals, grave-diggers, West Coast moist soil,
   his body passt four miles from me
along westering railway, unknown, dead, baggage,
   making twenty minute stop in the night,
here, thru Calgary, on way to West Coast rot,
   & he wont get up!   this is country
of silent wind piling drift snow in
      Rocky Mountains, trenches of quiet death,
      lonely desolation, long wind-silent drift,
   thru deep black space, fall, langorous drug,

      fading, falling sleep thru night of space,
smiling teeth, faint among stars, gone, night,
   gone, further, Ian, my friend, where are you?

The Oil

Sleepy old mind, I'm driving a car
across the prairie shivering under snow sky.
Old sky: I suddenly see with one rise of road
old buffalo fields,
                there is nothing
but buffalo turds on the grass
          from which we keep
          the home fires burning.

Alberta
          floats on a pool of natural gas
          the Peigans knew nothing of
          in their fright
          in their flight
             to the mountains.
                        We owe them that.

This straight line of highway
          & ghost wheat elevators
      everything here in straight lines
          except the Indian fields,
                    they roll
we say, rolling hills,
               but our things are
straight lines,
          oil derricks, elevators, train tracks
the tracks of the white man
               the color of
no white man, but
              dark as the earth
in its darkness,
          deep down oozing things:
I mean oil.

Alberta's unnatural heritage
concocted of Catholic adoption agencies
    &fundamentalist
    crooked coffee-stained neckties
at the expense of Indian boys,
    now Catholics with horses removed
from under them,
    the Peigans crosst the Rockies
to British Columbia
    where oil is more scarce
& people.
    In the high trees they rise now,
with campfire smoke,
    the smell of needles burning.

Buffalo shit smoke
    burning in Alberta
by the road, highway 2 North.

Now a
    Cadillac, I see a
    nother Cadillac, & there
is the black straight road, &
    a Cadillac,
    two Cadillacs
on the road, racing, North,
    the mountains to the left
blurred by a passing
    Cadillac.

Breaking Up, Breaking Out

Breaking up
of nations, sickness, log jam,
my psyche

the way of the world,
order,
form,

     as the body of a tree

grows outward
layer on layer, ring reaching
farther than previous ring–

This is the way
we break too

our strength, our hard bark
deflecting hard blows,
conducts the shock

inward.
A star of stress forms
cracks
moving to the surface.

Star I hang on,
my face showing nothing
at this age, twenty-eight,
encompassing all, showing
nothing

till the first crack.
That will appear
as my gracious gesture,

please, take this poem of love
as your own.

The Crumbling Wall

A crumbling wall
is a good thing,

it saves a city,
this kind of city,

pushing itself north
wall against new wall.

The foundation
is crumbling, that

is the only way
a community can build.

Let the bricks
fall out. A broken

wall is a thing of
beauty, for a certain

time. Joy does not
last forever. It

requires change, it
must crumble to remain.

Indian Summer

The yellow trees
along the river

are dying I said
they are in
their moment of life
you said.

The Indians I think
are dead, you cant

immortalize them, a
leaf presst between
pages becomes a
page.

In a month
the river will move

beneath ice, moving
as it always does
south. We will
believe it as we

will no longer see
those yellow borders
of the river.

The Cabin

Walking thru Banff woods
our arms held out in front
to hold off branches
from our faces

we came upon
the old mossy cabin
built by some man
now dead.

It was dark there, the trees
all around much taller
than they would have been
then.

Five hundred yards
from the highway
a cabin no one had lived in
all these years

stayed behind. We found
a deer skull
& took two teeth
to remember.

The Frost

But the morning
hoar frost

the breath of cold birds
on trees

the metal of January
in this place.

The crystals, white
hanging from the iron handrail

cold to fingers
sweet to taste.

Early Afternoon in the Rainy Season

Days like this
words are
lockt
inside somewhere

Across the street here
an old man in loose blue coveralls
sits under a dancing cactus
cutting weeds

The rain hasnt come
but heavy clouds fall
in the slopes of green hills

The loose trees
wave in the wind
& I

wave also, here on an ancient lake
south of the Tropic of Cancer
I wave

the flowers on the water
loose, caught & solidified
in the giant murals of the city
as I, before this Spanish typewriter
shaking my head to release words, flowers

the colors of Mexico,
pink cloth waving on a loose line
The old man is now
looking at the sky, his hand
touching his cactus

His words
hang in the air
before his face

Está Muy Caliente
(hace mucho calor)

On the highway
near San Juan del Río
we had to stop the car
for a funeral.

The whole town it was
a hundred people or
two hundred
walking slowly along the highway

toward the yellow domed church
on the top of the hill
& we pulled into the shade
of a shaggy tree.

I turned off the engine
& we heard their music
a screeching saxophone
& high broken noted trumpet

alone & sad in the hot afternoon
as they walkt slow like sheep
the women with black shawls
the men in flappy trousers.

Every five minutes the men
threw cherry bombs into the air
behind them: loud gun shots
blasting the afternoon

then the saxophone: tin music
odd tortured jazz
in that mysterious Indian Christian march
up the hill: bearing a coffin to the priest.

It was a small coffin
on the shoulder of one man in front
          the father we thought
the cherry bombs were like violence

against us: but we were stopt.
An old rattling truck
nosed thru them: & they closed
together again behind it
                              ignoring us.

I walkt away from the road
in among the bushes & prickly pear
looking for scorpions on the hot sand
& took a leak beside a thin horse.

An hour later the road was clear
& as I got in the car
a man on a donkey came by
a San Juan lonely in the mountains man.

Good afternoon, I said.
Good afternoon, he said, it is very hot.
Yes it is, I said, especially for us.
It is very hot for us too, he said.

Mexico City Face

The ninth month
of the Aztec calendar
is "the birth of the flowers"

the only time of year
men dance with women.

. . . .

Even the street lamp poles
have little faces carved
around them. Faces lost
in the city, so many of them.

The earthquake the night after
election day, shaking buried
Aztec bones under the city,
green flashes in the sky,

faces in the street, figures
dancing in green light, flowers
of night, election posters
flapping in the air.

The Aztecs used their stone
wheel to predict earthquakes,
the only wheel they had,
eathquakes & festivals, the birth
of the flowers.

                    & I
          enter this poem now, standing
          on the solid earth of Mexico,
          street lamps relit after the shifting
          is done. There is much earth
          under my feet, the city
          two miles above the sea. My face

          is lost in the city, this is not
          the ninth month, I stand only,
          I do not dance, my face
          sees another face high in the sky
          & under my feet there are
          buried bones come to rest.

Dolores Street Music

Ancient Aztec ashtray beside me,
I stop to remember

today 4 in the afternoon
on Calle Dolores
music at the door of the cantina

the musicians suddenly seen in the crowd
string bass dodging a parking car
guitar left hand high in the air
violin sawing Vienna into Alameda Park
&
    blind man clarinet:

sad music, music of uncontented groan
I also saw later in raggy man
lying on his hands in front of the store

the store woman stood over him
clapping her hands loud & yelling
but she turned to smile
this knowledge at passerby, customer, me
& the raggy man lookt up
with one eye

which I turned later to snow
July 9th snow on mountains far past
Calzada Ermita

sun on it, the mountain, clouds
drifting past, around its peak, fresh snow
I see from Mexico City, later

I am told that was the volcano, you
saw the volcano for the first time

& that sad uncontented music
rings the mountain, a break in the
rainy season

This ashtray, it was not an ashtray,
it was Aztec dish, the cigarette smoke
circles it.

The Beach at Veracruz

Your bare white legs
tight around the dolphin's back,

I see you dip below the wave
out of sight, to what world

of underwater castles, what
deep ride of deepening pressure
inside those thighs?

                    The beach
at Veracruz, after nightfall, is not
Mexico of my mind. Loose

German sailors sit at booze tables
eyeing the girls of strange language

two by two, large tits into
the noisy dance places. Sweat rolls

between their legs in those
tight clothes, & the air is
too tight, not Mexico air.

Men with frowning faces search
everyone entering those places, running

hands along their legs, looking
for concealed guns, everyone

is too fat here, the American
gun boats sit like steel offshore,

the only birds are fugitive, streaking
along the edge of sand, wings
silent in the dark.

& I am silent, sitting
on the wet sand at night,

looking east, to sea, at moon
light slicing between the waves,

or it is the cool gleam
of your naked legs, hundred yards
out there. I havent seen you

for minutes, you have finally
found your sea away from every-
thing.

      I stand, as you descend, no
doubt about it, you hold that

dolphin tight, as you hold your
breath, as I hold my breath. I

yell triumphant as your moonlit face
rides a wave out of the night

toward me, & your moon, your
thighs move two & two toward me.

Baseball,
a poem in the magic number 9
(for Jack Spicer)

1.

The white sphere
turns, rolls
in dark space

the far side of one destroyed galaxy,
a curve ball
bending thru its long arc
past every planet of our dream.

A holy spectre of a curve ball,
dazzling white, brand new
trademark still fresh:
"This is a regulation Heavenly League Baseball"

O mystic orb of horseshoe stitching!
Hurled from what mound in what Elysian field,
    from what mound, what
      mystical mount,
             where what life-bringing stream?

God is the Commissioner of Baseball.
Apollo is the president of the Heavenly League.
The Nine Muses, his sisters
       the first all-girls baseball team.
Archangel Michael the head umpire.
Satan was thrown out of the game
       for arguing with the officials.

In the beginning was the word, & the word was
"Play Ball!"

          Now that white sphere
          cools,
          & the continents
          rise from the seas.

          There is life
          on Baseball.

The new season is beginning.
Zeus winds up to throw out
the first ball
like a thunderbolt.

Take me out
          to the ball
                    game.

2.

July in Oliver, cactus drying
in the vacant lots,

in the ball park, the Kamloops Elks
here for a double header, Sunday

baseball day in Oliver, day of worship
for me.

          At the park an hour early,
scribbler full of batting averages,

sometimes I got a steel basket
& sold hotdogs, peanuts, sometimes

I pickt up a broken bat, lugged it home
& taped it, not so much for batting

as for my collection. Louisville Slugger.
My father was official scorer,

high in the chicken wire box
on top of the grandstand, he was tough

on the hitters, as later I was,
pens & pencils in front of me. Oliver

nearly always won, the cars parkt
around the outfield fence honking

for a hometown rally, me quieter,
figuring out the percentage, a third the age

of the players, calculating chances
of the hit & run play.

                    Later,
I was official scorer, they knew

I had the thick rule book memorized.
Sweat all over my face, eyes squinting

thru the chicken wire, preparing
batting averages & story for

the Oliver *Chronicle*.

3.

Manuel Louie, old Manuel Louie
is chief of the Indians around Oliver.
1965 now, he is 94, but he looks 55.
He's still got big black mustache, shoots pool
with his belly hanging over the rail.

Age 80, he was still playing Indian baseball games,
the chief, bowlegged running bases with turkey feather
in his hat.

The Wenatchee Chiefs, class A,
were spring training in Oliver then,
letting Manuel Louie work out at shortstop, weird Sitting Bull Honus Wagner,

in exchange for his steam bath, that's how he lookt 40
at age 80, a creek beside his house, mud hut full of steam.

That year the Wenatchee Chiefs finisht fifth.

4.

The New York Yankees
are dying this year, the famous pinstripe uniform
covered with dust of other ballparks.

Mickey Mantle is a tired man with sore legs,
working at a job. Roger Maris forgotten
on the sports pages, a momentary spark
turned to wet ash.

> A beanball on the side of the skull
> killed a ballplayer
> when I was a kid,
> it was violence
> hidden behind the grace of base-
> ball.

Now Warren Spahn is trying
to win a few more games
with his arm 44 years old,
in the National League
where no pitcher's mound
is Olympus.

& Willie Mays is after all
sinew & flesh
as a baseball
is string & leather,

& when baseballs get old
kids throw them around,
torn horsehide flapping
from that dark sphere.

       I was in love with Ted Williams.
       His long legs, that grace,
       his narrow baseball bat
       level-swung, his knowledge of art,
       it has to be perfect, as near
       as possible, dont swing
       at a pitch seven centimeters
       wide of the plate.

I root for the Boston Red Sox.
Who are in ninth place.
Who havent won since 1946.

It has to be perfect.

5.

In the nineteenth century
baseball came to the Pacific Northwest.

Mustache big muscled ballplayers of beer barrels
among bull lumberjacks & puffsteam train engines,
mighty trees of rainforest, pinstripe uniforms,
those little gloves of hurt hand, heavy bats of yore,
baseball in Seattles & Vancouvers of the past when Victoria
was queen of Canada, Manifest Destiny of the ballpark
cut into swathe of rainy fir trees.

Now still there—I go to see the Vancouver Mounties
of minor league green fence baseball playing
Hawaii of the Pacific, Arkansas Travelers of gray visitors garb,
I sit in warm sun bleachers behind first base
with Keep-a-movin Dan McLeod, bleach head poet of the Coast
gobbling crack shell peanuts—he's sitting beside me,
gadget bag full of binoculars & transistor radio, tape recorder,
cheering for the Mounties, nuts, they are Dominicans of the North,
dusky smiling on the lucky number souvenir program,
where I no longer write mystic scorekeeper numbers in the little squares,
sophisticate of baseball now, I've seen later famous players here.

> What are you doing, they ask,
> young esthete poet
> going to baseball games,
> where's your hip pocket
> Rimbaud?

I see the perfect double play, second baseman in the air legs tuckt
over feet of spikes in the dust, arm whipping baseball
on straight line to first baseman, plock of ball,
side's retired, the pitcher walks head down quiet from the mound.

6.

The herring-
bone stitching
takes one last
turn
till Louisville Slugger
        cracks
        & the spin
        changes, a cleat
                turns in the
                sod, digs earth,
                brown showing
                under green,
                bent knee takes
                pressure.

Lungs fill
with air,
pump-
action legs, foot
pounds on narrow
corner of the bag, rounding
                the body leans
                inward, eyes
                flick up once
                under cap, head
                down, legs running,
                buckle!

& the fire that breaks from thee then told a million
times
        since 1903,
        the first
        World Series, white sphere
        turns, the world again
        spun around once, the sun
        in October again sinking
        over the pavilion roof
        in left field.

This story is for you, Jack, who had eyes to see
a small signal
from the box
            more than 90 feet
            away.

7.

When I was 12 years old I had a baseball league
made of a pair of dice, old home-made scorebooks,
National Leagues, American Leagues, Most Valuable Players!

The St. Louis Browns played the Chicago Cubs in the World Series!
The Yankees finisht in seventh place, the batting championship
went at .394. It was chance, roll of dice, blood doesnt tell
in that kid's bedroom season—

                I was afraid to try out
                for the Oliver junior league team,
                I would strike out
                every time

                till I was sixteen,
                oldest you could be, & played
                one game before my summer job,

                & I hit a bases loaded single
                in the first inning. I was the
                tallest kid on the team.

But I bought Sport magazine & Baseball Digest, & knew all
the numbers. Ty Cobb's lifetime batting average was .367, I remember now,
Rogers Hornsby's lifetime batting average was .354. In 1921 Babe Ruth hit
59 home runs.

Ty Cobb was better than Babe Ruth.
Ted Williams was better than Joe DiMaggio.
I like the Boston Red Sox who are in 9th place.

I still play that game, I think.
I'm sitting at my desk in my bedroom right now.

8.

Nine.
Is a baseball number.
Nine innings.
Nine players.
Ted Williams was the best hitter of all time.
& the number on his back was nine.

Here is today's lineup:

lf	Terpsichore
2b	Polyhymnia
rf	Clio
1b	Erato
3b	Urania
cf	Euterpe
ss	Thalía
c	Melpomene
p	Calliope

A lineup like that is enough to inspire
the faithfulness of any fans of the good art
of baseball.

I have seen it happen
to the best poets
of this summer
& last.

9.

Long shadows
                fall across the infield
in the ninth inning.
                        Sometimes ball players
look like they're dying
                        as they walk off the field
in the dusk.

                I knew an old man in San Francisco
came to life
                when the Dodgers were in town.
Now he is dead, too,
                        & Jack is dead,
& the soldiers play baseball
                        in Asia,
where there is no season,
                        no season's end.

"It's just a game,"
                I used to be told,
"It isnt whether you win or lose,
                        but how you
play the game."
                In baseball
that is how you say
                the meek shall inherit
the earth.

                September 30, 1965,
Willy Mays has 51 home runs,
                        gray hair
at his temples,
                he says he has been
getting tired
                for six years.

I know I feel my own body
                    wearing down,
my eyes watch
            that white ball
coming to life.
            Abner Doubleday
lived in the nineteenth century,
                    he is dead,
but next spring
            the swing of a
35 ounce bat
            is going to flash with sunlight,
& I will be a year
            older.

My nose was broken twice
                    by baseballs.
My body depends on the game.
                    My eyes
see it now on television.
                    No chicken wire–
it is the aging process.
                    The season
can't help but measure.

                    I want to say only
that it is not a
            diversion of the intelligence,
a man breathes differently
                    after rounding the bag,
history, is there such a thing,
                    does not
choose, it waits & watches,
                    the game
isnt over till the last man's
                    out.

The House

1.

If I describe my house
I may at last describe myself

but I will surely lie
about the house.

For there is the first lie.
It is not a house at all

but a fragment, a share
of a house, instinct drives me

to one door. As certain as
one hair lies beside another.

As certain as these rows of books
carry me from house to house,

arrange me to their will. I
squat for an hour, eye level

to those books, saying I will
read this, or I will read this,

& this way never succeed
in reading my self, no time

left in the hour between
the news & the pants on the floor.

2.

In the morning the window
is bamboo & behind that

snow. (But here I am trying
to go outside the house, remember

what I said.) My bare feet
find no wood, the water

runs warm from the tap,
the coffee in the white cup

on which is painted a green
tree. There is a newspaper

on the floor inside the door,
& a woman in the chiffon

of the bed. A salt shaker
of glass & an aluminum

pepper shaker, & in the
farthest room, papers, orderly.

Those are the reason for the house
& its enemy. I am the fisher

who lays his fish side by side
in the pan. The noise of the pen

on paper is the drift of
cigarette smoke in the window's light.

3.

The house has a refrigerator
& a stove, a painting & a

husband, & the husband
has fingers from which words

fall as the wine glass falls
unbroken on the rug.

The key fits into the door
as my feet step in snow, cutting

precise patterns & the silence
of wind, & from outside

the windows are glass, &
behind that the house is not empty.

The Silence

The silence
that some days
brings itself between us

fools my heart,
it thinks there is
a loud constant noise.

The Boat

I say to you,
marriage is a boat.

When the seas are
high enough to
turn us over

we must hold
not one another
but our own positions.

Yet when the water
is calm under sea moon

we can even stand up
& dance
holding tight, each to each.

Windigo

Windigo
is twenty-five feet tall,
a long shadow
on the ice

& ice in him,
his heart,
made of hard ice.

He lives in the forest
of thin dark trees, north
where the sun
reaches on a slant,
casting long shadows,
                    the sun is too far
                    to reach that heart
                    of ice,
                    to melt it.

Windigo will eat a man
who loses himself
in the forest, he will
eat him without
killing the game,
ingest the scream
with the blood
that enters his own veins.

*

When Windigo meets Windigo,
male or female,
they do not mate,
they move closer,
their shadows cross,
& one dies,
body crashing with
crashing trees.

Then Windigo eats Windigo,
except the heart of ice,
which is crackt &
melted, water running
beneath the snow.

                    Arctic war
                    the elements
                    in deep ice
                    human form,
                    make arctic war,
                    simple, loud killing
                    & the bodies
                    consumed.

*

Windigo wears no clothes,
he is impervious to cold air,
he rubs resin from narrow pines,
& rolls in sand,
then stands, a rough statue
against the low sun,
long shadow on the ice.

Sometimes seen by dying birds
close to his mouth, a huge hole
in his face, without lips,
a ring of jagged teeth,
broken brown quartz, a deep
hole of stinking warm air
that hisses out,
     heard a mile away.

His huge round eyes
bulge out of his head, lidless eyes
rolling in red blood of pain,
always rolling, blood sockets
behind them.

    His feet, a yard long,
leave holes in the earth,
pointed heels & one bulbous
hairy toe, & his hands
are claws, brown & hairy,
ripping trees out of the ground
shaking earth from their roots.

His voice is thunder voice,
it rolls under clouds
of northern ominous weather,
& he howls in the night
& his howl melts the legs
of the man who runs before him.
    & his teeth
    gnash together
    jaggedly, an
    avalanche, it is
    terror.

*

He walks across the tundra,
tearing up trees in his way,
shaking earth from their roots,
& he enters tundra lakes,
making waves to turn over
canoes.

      In winter
he is always hungry, he eats
flesh, he eats rotten wood
from the ground, he eats
moss from the swamps, he eats
mushrooms, & he eats the hunter
who is in the forest after nightfall.

              Come home, hunter,
before nightfall, out of the forest
where Windigo is at your back,
he is hungry in winter,
his heart of ice drives him north,
his hands tear up trees
on your trail.

*

           To kill
Windigo, a silver bullet
into the heart of ice, or
the shaman's glassy stare
over his flames, no human
heart of blood can bring
that mountain to the ground.

Windigo,
            they say he was
once a man, winter
entered him, the wind
from the north in artery
to his heart, that ice, flow
thru his changing body.

They say the sorcerer
dreamt one night in north wind,
& the dream entered the forest,
& followed the hunter, finally
drank his heart.

            *

So sing to the Windigo
for mercy. Sing the shaman's song,
place food & drink, sacrifice
to the brother made beast,
the Windigo could be your brother,
he walks the forest at night,
screaming for your flesh,
sing the sacrifice song.

The song of the hunter,
the scream of the Windigo,
the heart of ice

            appears
in the chest of the man
who suddenly craves a man's flesh.
He must be a sacrifice too,
he must ask to be sacrifice,
he could be the Windigo of his brother,
his song can turn to scream of the ice heart.

& ice in him,
his heart,
made of hard ice.

> Come home, hunter,
> before nightfall,
> your brother is Windigo.
>
> The heart of ice
> was heart of blood,
> winter
> has entered him.

So sing to the Windigo for mercy,
your brother,
sing the shaman's song,
& sing for your own heart too.

Hamatsa

1.

The poet among us said
the west coast is unknown,
a bird in the rain.

There is Matem, occupying
the top of a new mountain,
a large bird with eyes for
the hunter who wishes
to fly.

                      The poet among us
has flown, in solitude
to the near mountains. The
mountains in the sea
where the sun goes down
& raises the tide.

But I have seen
Baxbakualanuxsiwae
at the mouth of the river
disgorging into the straits,
& his bird
Qoaxqoaxualanuxsiwai, the raven
who eats the eyes.

The wise man's eyes
are in his head, said
the poet among us, I have seen
into my sea of changes, it
is inside me, & the book
I read below the mountains.

The Kwakiutl boy
who would eat the flesh
of his people must meet Baxbakualanuxsiwae
at his house where blood red smoke
rises to the sky, blood
dissipated in the blue there.

Only a few in many may
eat human flesh, & swallow the sea.

& Baxbakualanuxsiwae has two women,
Oominogu his wife, bringer of corpses,
& Kingalalala, her servant.
& the birds, said Qoaxqoaxualanuxsiwai
the eyeball-eater, & Hoxhok
with long beak for skull brains.
& also the grizzly bear,
called Haialikilal.

Here at Kitsilano Beach, we gather
driftwood to pile & burn
bonfires, the long sky color of the sea.
The poet among us speaks of mountains.
Where snow is Chinese, the warm house
full of wise words, far from the shore.
& his head is a house
of wisdom, warm inside bone.

The Kwakiutl youth aspires
to become Hamatsa, the elite,
his patron Baxbakualanuxsiwae,
in a word, he-who-may-eat-human-flesh,
four pieces at a time,
to swallow without chewing,
then disgorge with swallowed sea water.

The poet among us goes to the University
of British Columbia, on Spanish Banks,
a forest of dead sailors.
Where the industrial smoke of higher learning
rises to the sky, merging with cloud.

> "A man must have care
> from word to word,
> not to go soft
> or his life will go soft"
> he says, in the fire-glow.

Clouds, meanwhile, loom up
from Japan's ocean, the air turns cold,
the beer makes us shiver.

Matem gets up on his wings,
lifts himself to the next mountain.
Hamatsa stalks the forest
looking for a burial-tree.

2.

I am a new voice now—
this is Hamatsa—
& I want to say
what I have is
a fucking awful job.

Let me tell you:

I wear the mask & dance the dance
of dead Baxbakualanuxsiwae
I met on the mountain,
& my sister sits among the women.
She does not know me.
No hot stones for my feet.
& that is not so bad.

Hap! Hap!
My sister fears me, the cry
I learned in the forest,
Hap! Hap!
She must be my Kingalalala,
she will bring me flesh
from tops of trees,
torn between her fingers
for my legend.

The men fear me too, it is why
I became Hamatsa,
I move among them,
biting flesh from their
arms & chests.

They come to me with the rattles
dancing, crying Hoip! Hoip!
to ease me in their direction,
telling me whose meat to devour,
which way to make their
politics.

Later, in my cabin I receive
the old Hamatsas, with the flesh
from trees, saying
"These are my travelling provisions,
Baxbakualanuxsiwae himself
has brought me."

My sister serves the meat
unwillingly, places it on the drum
no hands touch, & the the old Hamatsas
dance their pretended frenzy
to that music.

Then: begin.
My sister takes four mouthfuls
of the flesh,
between each, a drink of sea water.
& after her
each of the old Hamatsas,
four mouthfuls, whole flesh,
not to be chewed with the teeth.

& myself, four mouthfuls,
down to the sea, the sea water
makes me retch, horrible
in the stomach—
the ugly faces,

my sister,
retching.

You must not keep the flesh.

Hap! Hap! Hap! Hap!
We face the sunrise,
dipping four times
under salt water.

This is to be elect, a
Hamatsa, blessed by the monster
on the mountain, a fucking
awful way to live.

Not as hero to the people,
but servant.
It is so
complex.

For the rest of my life
to walk from hut to hut,
wearing their bark,
dancing to their music,
eating whatever they serve me,
whatever shit.

Very romantic for the man
who wanted to eat human flesh.

Even to drink water,
I dip my bowl three times in the stream,
& swallow four mouthfuls of water
thru the eagle's wingbone,
my lips inviolate,
man-eating lips.

I cannot scratch bugs from my hair
with my fingers, but carry another bone.
These bones–these limitations.
It is not art, but politics.

3.

Right now, you're all expecting me
to perform for you, say something
witty
said the poet among us.

Let me tell you
something–

4.

The first Hamatsa started this way,
& what follows is transliteration
of Kwakiutl legend:

In the dark backward & abysm of time
they first encountered
Baxbakualanuxsiwae.

Nanwaqawe, the chief
had of his wife four sons, big thighed
walking mountains, hunting goats
on the edges, high above the water.

They came home because they were
sons of the chief, but others
went to the mountains & never came home,
& their women said
we shall have no more men.

Only Nanwaqawe knew of
Baxbakualanuxsiwae,
in the mountains where the goats were.
But he was chief, it was his tribe
of the women.

He called together his sons,
Tawixamaye,
Qoaqoasililagilis,
Yaqois,
Nulilokue,
to speak—he said
go into the mountains, my sons.

& when you come near to a house on the mountainside
the smoke of which is red like blood, do not enter,
or you will never return home. It is the house of
Baxbakualanuxsiwae.
Do not enter the other house on the mountainside
the smoke of which is gray on one side; for that is the house of
the grizzly bear, Haialikilal. Harm will befall you
if you enter that house. But now go, my four sons,
& keep wide your eyes as you go,
or you will not return.

Early next morning they saw the house of the gray smoke.
& the eldest, Tawixamaye, said
this is the house of the grizzly,
we will see him whom our father alone knows.

They saw blood & flesh dripping
from the yellow fangs. High in the doorway.
Kwakiutl blood, man flesh. The women
weep, men fight. Let us slay this bear
said Tawixamaye.

The black bird with bent wings high in a tree
watcht them all day round the bear,
their wounds dripping
till the sun fell behind the ocean
& Tawixamaye's club smasht the high skull
& the bear lay at their feet,
blood dripping on him.

Come, said the killer, our journey into the mountains
is not yet over.

In the dark they walkt, dark of large crooked wings,
till Nulilokue the youngest dropt with his wounds
& they slept till another sun
came free of the mountains.

& walkt until they saw the great pillar of red smoke
red like blood, rising into the blue heavens, it was the house of
Baxbakualanuxsiwae.
We will see him whom our father alone knows
said Tawixamaye, the eldest son.

The sky murky over their heads, blood from the fires
of Kwakiutl flesh, they ran to the door,
the killing club banged there, on the door, there
was no answer, till they opened the door,
dead grizzly behind them, into the darkness within.
Full of smoke, & a woman's voice.

Said help me, I am rooted to the floor,
help me, then I may help you, whom I long awaited.
The women's voices wept behind them.
What? said the four brothers. What?

See nothing when the smoke clears,
see nothing, dig
a deep hole in the floor, place stones
in this fire, when they are red-hot
place them in the hole,
cover the hole with boards, it is for
Baxbakualanuxsiwae.

The sun went dark, a great whistling came thru the forest,
the monster stood at the doorway, crying
Hap! Hap! Hap! Hap!, water pouring from his mouth
like a woman's weeping.
& Hoxhok & Qoaxquoaxualanuxsiwai the birds
cried Hap! Hap! Hap! Hap!

                    In the forest
                    the small animals trembled.
                    The trees moved
                    their branches.
                    The rabbit screamed.
                    The rabbit screamed.

5.

The west coast is unknown,
a small bird in the fog.

The poet among us
remembers great piles of clam shells
where the river was,
part of a skull
buried under old refuse,
a deserted town
two thousand years old.

6.

A giant stood in the tall doorway,
the four brothers felt cold shadow on them,
their sun gone dark, the woman quiet behind them,
rooted to the floor.

Baxbakualanuxsiwae lay now on the floor.
They saw his body covered with blood-stained mouths,
gaping teeth all over him.

Baxbakualanuxsiwae now stood up,
walking around in the smoke, crying
Hap! Hap! Hap! Hap!

The raven danced in his feathers
before the fire of blood smoke,
& the other bird, dancing, joined
the three with their screams & bloody mouths,
& the women, the wife & the slave,
crying Hoip! Hai! Hai! Hai! Hai!
While in the valley the women wept quietly.

Till the giant thumping feet of
Baxbakualanuxsiwae pounded near the covered hole
so quickly the eldest brother snatcht away
the boards, & the monster danced down into the hole,
his feet jumping from red-hot rocks.
Quick, bury him! screamed the woman rooted to the floor.
& the three brothers flung rocks, to cover him.

& now Baxbakualanuxsiwae was dying.
His meat steamed & hisst,
his red smoke joined the blood smoke of his chimney,
hole in the roof, sky outside, to the clouds, blood-red.
Where the two birds vanisht while
the woman died, no more screaming, silence of smoke
filled the house.

7.

Oh, fish, what are you doing at the bottom of the sea,
said the poet among us,

& we all lookt out over the water,
Vancouver harbour,
to where the sun burnt out red
between two mountains.

I am given to understand this, he said,
that eating human flesh is a dull job,
like the navy, it seems adventurous
beforehand.

Under the ocean fish eat one another,
& they are carried by heavy currents
to & fro,
noses in front of them.

8.

Now said the woman rooted to the floor,
take these things from this house,
they once belonged to
Baxbakualanuxsiwae:

> ornaments of red cedar bark,
> mask,
> whistles,
> totem pole, it is the Hamatsa pole,
>
> & the Song
> of Baxbakualanuxsiwae.

But Tawixamaye the eldest brother
said this belongs to our father, the chief
heard the news of the story, at dawn
began the climb of the mountain with his four sons.

Where they found the old house, red smoke
still rising, death in the air, rising,

an old man met the woman rooted to the floor,
& she said:

> Now you shall dance,
> With the cannibal mask,
> the mask of Hamatsa,
> among you, dance,
> but first I will teach you
> the Song.

> & she sang.

Who are you, askt the old man,
& she laught a terrible laugh:

> You do not know
> who I am?
> I am your daughter,
> Baxbakualanuxsiwae
> did not devour me,
> but rooted me to the floor
> to mock me till
> the end of time.

Then the old man rejoiced.
We will take you with us & feast
& the women will weep no longer, he said,
& he smiled.

> I cannot move, I
> am rooted, she said.

So they set to digging, but the deeper they dug
the wider was the root, & they dared not cut it,
their sister was a part of the earth.

Who said:

> You must return to the river,
> to make the Winter dance,

                    let my brother, Tawixamaye
                    disappear, he will become
                    Hamatsa, the Cannibal,
                    & later let my brother, Qoaqoasililagilis
                    disappear, he will be
                    Qominoqa the food-gatherer.

                    Thenceforward let Hamatsa
                    do no work, or he will die early.

& so it was, the Winter feast, & later
Hamatsa, of the mask, of the
flesh,

a fucking awful job.

9.

Curious, on the west coast, we all
feel that appetite, the poet among us,
one of them, never sees himself
but as dancer among us, preferred
                    position, must do no work

                    or he will die young.

                    The sun falls at last
                    behind offshore islands, the sky
                    is red as pale blood,
                    we all on the beach, walk
                    across the sand, dancing
                    on the old shifting earth,

                    the sand is eroded mountains,
                    sky is full of the sea,
                    our flesh full of the flesh of others,
                    voices reflecting off the same trees.

Hamatsa
the cannibal, down off the mountain
hidden in the forest of our eyes.

The Egg

The egg sat on the workbench
for weeks, me passing it every day
in my search for tools, cobwebs,
five years old, looking for

the machines of life. The source
of life, I knew, as mysterious as
my mother's bedroom. I didn't touch
the egg for weeks, my brain resembling

its contours. Till the day came
I gave up waiting for the news, I
contrived to make it roll & fall
to the floor beside a rusted shovel.

Bending over, I knew first the
terrible stink, & then the quills
of light, bone, or fiber, it was
a wing never to be used. It's guilt

I carried for a year & then carried
lighter for more years, as if I
myself smelled, as if I had brought
those tender stinking wings to earth.

Dobbin

(*for Mike Ondaatje*)

We found dead animals in our sagebrush hills
every day it seems now, deer, heads of
unimaginable elk. Or rattlesnake killed
by some kids we likely knew, upside down,
wrong colored in the burnt couchgrass.

But my first dead horse. It was something
like mother, something gone wrong at home—
his opened & scattered body was tethered,
the old shit surrounded his tufted hair
& his skin, the oil gone, just twisted
leather without eyeballs. A horse, as if
someone had lost him, obeying the rope
thru his open-air starving.

I was then, then, no longer another one
of the animals come to look, this
was no humus like the others, this
was death, not merely dead; that rope
may now hang from some rotted fence.

Grass, Grass

A clogged ashtray a dead lung,
old fish on a plate,
drear classrooms I enter & re-enter
saying next life I'll eat oranges every day–

. . . .

Let me speak to you
as before me I was spoken to:
remember to lie on the grass of cold morning,
not dreaming but eyes open where they hurt
with the cold & the morning,
not commanding the sun,
not communing with the soil,
but wearing any shoes, any serviceable coat,
hands in pockets for the dew
of a finisht & unimportant night.

Then drive your car if you will
back onto the drying streets,
but merrily, merrily, & if you will,
remembering me, remembering that I spoke
even from collapsing lung,
even with raw-bitten fingers on your arm.

That I was allowed to say this,
that I intend to say it,
all the dew of morning remember, & the mist
that catches light before you see sun,
that is no longer night of unimportance,
that living fish are stirring in their water,
& dogs bark, seeing their breath,
& bark at their visible breath,
& that is to look at, smile or no,
that I
do not bark now,
I am not barking to no purpose,
I am not barking,
I am not a man barking.

As I am allowed to speak,
be there no morning, no walk.

I tell you as I was told,
you may even leave an orange outside the door overnight,
suitable to eat cold
even while you lie on the grass,
& its color orange,
& its color green.

I Said I Said

I said I said.

At the first glance you see there a singleness of intention,
to make the overly familiar
less exotic
to wash
it
away.

I was kicking the sea furiously,
bringing down fat smelly birds with a glance,
glamorizing my supper &
forcing it down too, it

all went down them days, even
with my friends who suspected
a frail bird of a large sort
inside that flesh, wings wet,
sagging. With bright bright eyes.

So I even managed to tell myself I wasnt faking when I sat at the table late
at night in Oliver & told my mother I'd rob her or anyone else to do my
writing. She thought of it as a hobby, an evening thing for a teacher, an
illusory abberation at least at first. Later a source of some balm among the
irritation.

A glance, one glance
at the real world would have saved so much time

but it was happily spent despite the railing
(the stage again)
against its ravages, that indulgence when yr young.

I'll learn to do without birds
except where I fail at photographing them
or eat bits of them on occasion.

That is the gentle meal, not
talking too much yrself, waiting to hear
he said.

About I.

Poem Written for George (1)

Poetry with politics in it
is small men answering back to volcanoes.

Volcanoes are upside down grails
knights look for
walking on their hands.

I never met a poet yet
who was a knight.

Knights are ignorant men with strong arms.

I never met a soldier yet
who was a poet.

Poets dont look for grails.

They want to drink from
the cups at hand.

Sometimes they climb mountains
to look down the middle
where mangled kings lie in a heap.

Poem Written for George (2)

To pass a mirror
without composing
before it

is to lose
is to lose.

We all win too much
for our own good.

Making pictures
where there were faces.

Look
I can make the dew
dry on the trees.

I can carve wood
into a likeness
of my father.

I can burn thru cloud
& wood, given time.

Awful gift.

Give us rather fingers
for all our veils.

Give us the dissolving fabric
we may dare to put on.

Let us for ourselves find
a face that looks at us still
for all our moving.

Round Head

Why given round heads
if not for immortality?
        I dont want
to come on mysterious, I'm speaking
of shapes, our world we move
our shapes among, growing, waning,
wavering before what forces
inside & out,
behind & before,
              in wandering lines
or circles that suggest
eternity. That is the head, the
actual head, the organic bone
is infinite circles grown together
not to die a husk,
but at least to hold one star
in its dry void.

Talent

Not to have pity for objects
because they are dumb,
not to have sympathy
for their suffering,
is talent–

but beginning with respect.
To love what is your choosing
not as a political
move, but specific, to say

"I love you" is as
a knife wound, not to be
shaken around, but to
hold together
            with wet lips.

There is talent as
implemented. The "work" of art
nearly swallowed, elemental
as a baby's mouth
that opens not in love
but out of need.

                That
is when I say
I love you, that

is when I feel talent
down my arms, into
my fingers,
            when I can
lay myself before any pity,
uncaring.

No Time Left

1.

What can happen to you
& to you, & to them, my
other yous, in the years left

as I begin to write, wondering
what is beyond the world's
circle of air, coming this way

intent not on us, but coming
to rules, laws, our rules
we feel in our blood, the fluid

of our eyes so short of sight.

2.

Perceiving the other-side of everything
is work of the decent soul

so difficult, the brain saying
this is me, my center

cortex around which electricity
hums–that must be

loosened–lessened, a lesson
learned, we try

I say, yearn, for the brother
lost at birth, it is us

for myself I speak, it is I
I encounter in back of the

authentic, behind my eyes, a
universe of souls, happy with

one another, knowing the future
as shared, as everywhere
the real

manifests itself in the colors
of the present, only half

perceived, the other half
available to the soul that will

venture, say bring the future
our gift

the book this universe sets us
to read.

Let us read, you & you &
them, my other yous, let us

sit down & read
together.

3.

Of certain things that bear
shapes out of the future:

the oval pebble of the river
the white rose
& the white rose worm
the oblate skull of your daughter
the glistening back
of my beloved, under me.

Throw the clocks from the window
& the rings of your fingers
& the fingers with them,

watch them fall forever
in moonlight, fall yourself
upward.

4.

I had meant to speak of the future.

We say clouds, a fog, the
veils & curtains, a gauze
thru which to see dimly,

but it is also a vast clarity
not lookt upon
because inward, no anxious eye
looks inward.

        My chromosomes
once yours, carry the news
of a million futures
that combined make a fragment
too small to care for.

Your fingers on my waist
count more, count on your fingers.

They point the way
to the future.

5.

Women spend much time in the past
& when I enter you I am
giving myself in care to
what has been, & is
turning in your mind, & yours.

Am I a scholar of time
to be telling this to you
while I lie on the sweat of your belly?

I know time races
as your breath comes faster

& there is no time
afterwards.

The future lies behind us, yes
behind us.

Play Among the Stars

Every noon
I cook two eggs

seeking the variations
that speak of

a higher galaxy
in any menial action

done right, done
with grace, done

as lovely as these two
sunny side up.

Pharoah Sanders, in the Flesh

Walking east on 3rd street
to listen to Pharoah Sanders
I have to step around rotting junk,
wearing my sorcerer's gloves,
blue, orange, red & gray

to enter out of fear, short
of breath, into Slugs' bar, warm
as crowded bodies can make it,
warming the small mugs of ale.
warming already to the unfamiliar

setting to be welcomed as the new
familiar, as Japan played in Africa
on vinyl, in Quebec. This is my first
encounter east of Avenue B,
having given up my money, my coat,

my Kanadian white face, knowing
they dont know I've heard that music
for years in my best friends' blood-
streams; I look for the face
on my typing room wall, he's there,

Pharoah, fey row, little boy lost
leaning on the wall of the little stage
banging two tambourines together,
legs bent & straightening, coming
northeast from Arkansas, east again

to Sun Ra's bar & his continent
laid open by the Nile. We arent far
from the East River, the slug
floating heavily to the sea. I've
got a seat, Pharoah Sanders

has pickt up his magnificent horn,
chasing these warmed up pictures
from my mind; I've come out of
literature, right into the roar
of that belly's horn, I wish I could

just run up & grab him &
stop saying that's Pharoah Sanders,
that's really Pharoah Sanders.

Dec.1968

Single World West

(Bring it to you
or get right into it,

it is not a world parallel
to your own)

Have questions.

Would I have shot
John Wesley Hardin,
given the chance?

Two.

Would I have shot him
in the back
or dared him in sunlight,
thinking of the literature?

(When we stood on Custer's knoll
we stood, god damn it, where
men got their balls cut off,
where scared privates with children
lay with empty rifles
& arrows go in a foot deep)

Would I have hated Wild Bill Hickock
for being a drunk bully,
for killing his friend in panic,
for beating the shit out of women?

I could have been in Deadwood
among 20,000 criminals
a thousand miles from law,
where a dirty drunk American
might take it into his head
to point his gun at me
for being quiet & thoughtful.

(It is not a parallel fictitious world,
we haven't got away from it.

Did Kennedy ask himself those questions?

The radio is not a parallel universe,
its messages are real as your brain)

What would you do
if your god told you
to kill his enemies for gain?

Right now
are you wishing I had more control
over my material?

(If you are not into it yet,
keep trying. Love & history
are like each other.

                        Be willing
to be carried closer. Lovers
are not parallel)

Three.

Would I want magic
in a poem about
killing John Wesley Hardin?

George Custer thought
his legend controlled his fate,
Crazy Horse rubbed his pony
with magic stones.

When they hit each other
it was not in literature,
it was in this single world,
my friend.

June 5/68

Ike & Others

1. form

Do not
      fill an order,

that is commerce, & especially
do not
      fill an order
made from yr own choosing, that

is a rule of procedure.

Look instead to laws,
where they come from, not
where you might go to complete
obligations, especially again

as made by yr own boss, appointed
by you, that illogical the rational
rootless
        mind, uptorn from the earth

as you must never be save
as metaphor, for moving, to get there
to the source,
          to look

at the rest of you.

        That is
put yr ear to yr pulse,
or let yr breath fall on the back of yr hand.

2. *content*

              Be content.

& be of use or example,
as the trees you sing so sweetly of
are hurt under the keys of yr typewriter.

The hands you see caressing the bark of that pine
might be equally on yr own trunk,

you are as much a marker in the music
be you singer as well,
                    have you listened to the tree?

(Once when Ozark Ike misst a fly ball
& crasht into the fence, game over, his body
stretcht there, the trainer said
where does it hurt?

Ike said up there, looking at the scoreboard.)

3. *place*

Ike's bat is made from an ash tree,
which has been compared to a man.

Ike's glove is made from a cow,
which is thought to be man's servant,
& gives its teats to his child's mouth.

The game Ike plays is thought to be
pure ritual.

It is a matter of,
                    for instance,
cities, how I learned them,

Boston,
Chicago,
St Louis,
Pittsburgh,
wrongly, but to some extent.
                    It is only later
on entering them I see
the inner city of Detroit is a worn out floor above another
surrounding the stadium.

Is this how a kid from New York
mistakes a mountain valley in the far west?

4. *community*

& those kids have made a truce,
no polis,
a deal with unknown citizens
& their captors.

My sister's skin is strange to me,
I live among similar minds
at best
at the far reaches of my thought.

If I sit on a horse
it is in imitation
of a cowboy
trying to bat .300.

5. *work*

"but if you do not even understand what words say,

how can you expect to pass judgement
on what words conceal?"

6. *words*

What would you like to call that?
said God,
& Adam said it looks like a horse, I'll
call it a horse.

He is yr servant, said God,
I made all these things
in the last 5 days, now
yr the boss,

name them & they're yrs.

But how can I arrive at a name
without asking them
if they already got secrets, said Adam.

You are Man
said God.

Moses tells us all this, & Moses
was also boss.

Power corrupts, said the golden calf.

Smash that son of a bitch, said Moses,
not remembering Adam said a bitch
was a dog, man's best servant.

But Moses had a speech impediment, remember,
his brother spoke for him,
he carried messages carved in stone,
he was too hung on power to be a poet
like David
before David decided to be king.

7. *signs*

But we dont carry stone tablets
as our sign, our words

are not to prescribe behavior.
Polis

is not layered, power
corrupts

save that secret power
we plug in-to,

where we find our emblems,
a reed, a round stone, a ring

& a ring of
something like electricity,

not at our service, not
at our switch, the finger

bends only to grasp,
to caress, for instance, the tree.

The Owl's Eye

Angela sits & wishes
we could see
the pictures on the wall.

Another lady saw
such vision
& made the best poems
of our time.

I hope they meet,
those two, silently,
seeing each other
as angels introducing
marvelous beasts.

An owl with eyes
in whose
iris grow the flowers
of wisdom.

She sat outside as well
& heard the song-
birds for the first
time.

They rime to the music
in the center
of all liquid, blood
& the fluid of the
wide open eyes.

Earlier she wrote
of the other lady's
visitation. Her words
were then as now

to direct us
to the wings, to the
secrets seen in the grain,
to the pictures
they seem to write.

Mars

1.

One lion got away
from Mr Hemingway

& walks in here
discernible by his red
eye.

It shines like a
bank of flame, united.

The lion sits, king
of beasts, god
to some men,

those warriors who
kill him with
their spears

& never water
their dry earth
with their tears.

2.

Two moons make
for various light,

a shadow for instance,
in a shadow. No lion

would stand for that,
coming in to sit down,
king cat.

A corby sat
on either side of the twig

waiting to eat
the red light
of those eyes.

Under the light
of the moon

where my boots
hold me up
& shine.

3.

Three-legged stools
offer stability

for those who sit.
The triangle sounds lovely

but the stress hurts
at the corners.

The warrior remembers
pain, magic is for

outsiders never near
the blade.

       The lion
sits on his three-legged stool

4.

remembering the whip.
It looks like magic

save from his fiery
eye.

Four from the sun
he spins, his moons

spinning about him, their light
always in his red eye.

All my life I've been told
what he will look like

thru the glass, so I
have never laid
my eye there.

So I have never relinquisht
my lions, prancing
beside their canals.

5.

Five is the number
in the painting, a

handful of paint.
This picture of

what I myself can hold,
whip or chair

to hold the cat
at bay. Fingers to

touch holes in the flute

as well.

6.

Six & seven, at sixes
& sevens, the lion

sat before his book,
fixing our disorder

with his look.
He told me later

I hold a whip too,
a world is mine

three from the sun.

Tomorrow, I replied, the moon
will blink the sun,

& wars will stop
to be revived in its light.

7.

Seven years after
his claw raked my face

in a dark Vancouver room
the lion appeared

to embrace me, his eye
blazing red

in another room. The war
is still
being waged,

the lines are drawn
differently.

March 1-7/70

Touch

1. *touches*

Myself among the particles, multitudinous.
Not to be measured
but counted only, among the realizations
that all touch
                will be shared, the particles
seizing or caressing, me.

One.

Another.

& yet

another.

2. *in finding the perfect melody you would encounter the perfect law*

Inchanting, yes,
when I measure it is not to find
my capacity, fear finding of that always

but look around, see the very lineaments
of the bowl, this sky, where
I also float while it fills

always to be drained.
& the measuring is of particles,
myself one of many, or many

as you are my dear, dear to me
for your numbers or your numbering among
indeterminate many. Or few.

                Or when I look back on this
                I see I may have said we are both
                rain, & find our function there,

inchanting, the melody & the law
to make the grass grow la de daw.
I am so serious I am driven to play–

(We may do no more than
deliver the law, my dear, as the melody
delivers ourselves here measuring

sweetly, not comparing you to me
or me to other. It's never amateur night.
We chant by chance, eye on a lovely light

from the stars, from the poet of the stars,
from the animal bedevilled by the stars,
from a crown glittering starlight, I mean starlike.)

Always to be drained, tipt
over, entered that way, filled & drained
of love, the measurement by the rod

flowering, my name made lovely, the sentence
lost in a maze meant for delight, the lost there
finding the measure of each other in inchantment.

3. *chop down the poison tree*

Okay call me a nature poet
darling reviewer or whoever
you are, you are yourself the root & trunk
of my rime, you Indian hiding inside.

4. *choices*

Even choosing the yellow & blue pen
from the bamboo cup
                          is another touch
as I "see" it,
              all the while
losing your ear while I listen for
deeper music.

              You in the other room
studying, words
              of Carlyle who said music
lies at the heart of every thing
                                or I
said it, lying as always & even now,
the pen I often write about
merely a machine in the hand of a machine?

              (To get closer—
              the question mark
              begs the question)

There are no choices as we remember events.

There are events we may choose in the future
to describe
              as co-ordinate.

              We long so for order.

5. *in the district*

Dont tell me electricity
depends on touch, electricity

depends on no strength but a weakness
accomodated, a gap filled.

The air, she said, was electric
between them, ready to make a pun on con-
duct.

      But that poet's emanations
were kosmik, as the vulgar say,

vibrations—the kosmos is free
from electricity. Speak to me of energy.

I hold with that. But electricity
is only a gesture, made because we are near
& nearby.

6. *scars*

What kind of touch was that,
    the gash our lady Jesus
        exposed for the doubting finger of Thomas?

It was likely the newly moistened
    wound of Adam
        whence she came, a rib like a spear.

That split pulsing within
    with a sympathetic rhythm
        of the kosmos.

that we feel, running our fingers
    over the scars, that sweet flesh
        joined over the gone appendix.

A useless organ now, they say,
    the surgeon's objective touch
        more gentle than God

with none of Tom's uncertainty.

7. *the citizens*

    Barrientos' helicopter hit the wires
& fell into the jungle,

                     more metal insect scrap
laced with meat
            like the peeled birds of Viet Nam,
in sight of dark eyes
               above drooping rifles.

That kind of touch too,
              or those—
steel on earth, clumsy,
            the connections

across Pacific Ocean, where
      the raftsmen floated.

                  All green
the foliage, the slack uniforms,
            the
eventual buzzing of the color TV
      finding it, among shadows

of a green
      too deep to touch at all.

8. *adam's finger*

    In all the corners of every continent
of Men we come upon their streets
    & the walls dead fingers have toucht.

The man who died
in the bed where my father sleeps
also walkt
in streets my boots search out
far from his telling.
The poor shoes
I wore at his funeral
only pulp of the earth
now, even the photograph beginning to fade
as the blue of my father's eye
lightens.

Brightens, as I look out from it
to where three presidents
have disappeared today
(as my early poem
disappears into what library).

Barrientos, O'Neill, de Gaulle
who walkt their streets in the clothing
of powerful men afraid
to dress in new ideas every day.

What the dead man last said to me
is forgotten.
What the other said
as the machine fell to treetops
is history
falsified.

I dont mean to say
a slate may fall on you tomorrow,

that is touch
you may weigh in your mind.
I mean to say
more. & I will
given the chance,
I mean given clearance
to walk down your street
made as much
by your name
on a younger man
waiting to inherit your empty clothes,
the avenues you cut & wear,

the eyes you brighten with your
ideas so quickly mistaken,
so slowly worn,
mister prime minister.

9. *inches*

& I find it is by fingers
we measure to begin with
an inch at a time,
the rule of thumb.

I find that each of my fingers
bears a scar
being broken one by one.

I'd forgotten my ounce of prevention
is an inch measured
once too late,

but my fingers now
touch, each singly with their histories
connected by blood,

connected by what is mainly water.
                    An inch is also an island.

10. *sentimentality*

    Now my skin feels the touch
                that is not a touch, perhaps
        only a memory of what was truly
                not quite a touch.

Or how can I hope to give you
        a morning before driving 500 miles
            between small western towns?

    The front windows of eastern houses
                    are small, only sunk in the wall
differently from back windows.

                            Our windows opened
to sage & dust & roads with weeds down the middle
            & birds that lay in the wind
    with wings only flicking momentarily.

    Outside eastern windows the birds
                hop crookedly between twigs.
                    Or they wear 3-piece suits.

& when I see the birds at last
    I take up their wind
        & want to drive, west

    where I imagine the sun to be going
                finally to touch down
                        in dry grass where its breadth
    needs those wide windows.

11. *the cup, though*

We break the laws one by one
to keep in touch,
              not to be broken
    to the final inch.

Some like our lady Jesus
finally jambed against wood pulled from its earth
      giving its water, giving his blood
        to encircle a larger island.

Many more testing smaller resources,
      measuring with smaller cups,
       waiting shorter times
    to watch them fill,

        while every day the sky fills
   describing itself not as law,
     neither as melody, but turning
to empty & fill, empty & fill,

     leaving it for me to name
them cups, fingers, wounds, melodies,
   never to be left,
         but left
to look at this hand,
       filled with blood–

when I cease writing, I turn it over,
       & it is a vessel.

12. *speech*

To annoy my wife
   I touch tongues with the dog
& only later adopt
     a deeper meaning.

Not God merely in bread,
remember, & not just good breeding
in man or familiar.

Touch demands that, extension,

& what demands touch?

I lost many people
by my satisfaction to love them inwardly,
at least partially.
The leper, what use
to touch him, to demonstrate
with mortal finger given once by God?

It's only that she will touch that tongue later,
& I cant blame her,
it will also fall to her
to close my eyelids finally

& the dog will be dead many years.

But his life so short,
who is to say whose tongue that is?
what we feel, our fingers
gentle on the tiny bones of his ankles?

They resemble the parts of the tree
I dont see at first
or fully the unseen

in the other-half of the tree.

See? she says:
I turn, & she is holding the new plant,
its flowers finally there
inside the open window.

Other Books by GB

Sticks & Stones (1963)
Points on the Grid (1964)
The Man in Yellow Boots (1965)
The Silver Wire (1966)
Mirror on the Floor (1967)
Baseball (1967)
Rocky Mountain Foot (1969)
The Gangs of Kosmos (1969)
Two Police Poems (1969)
Sitting in Mexico (1970)
George, Vancouver (1970)
Al Purdy (1970)
Genève (1971)

This book was designed by David Shaw.